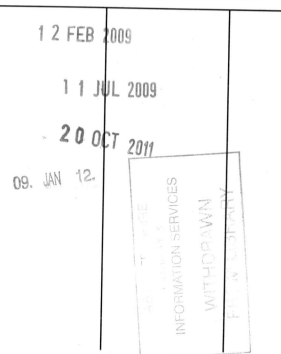

Editorial consultant: Mitch Cronick

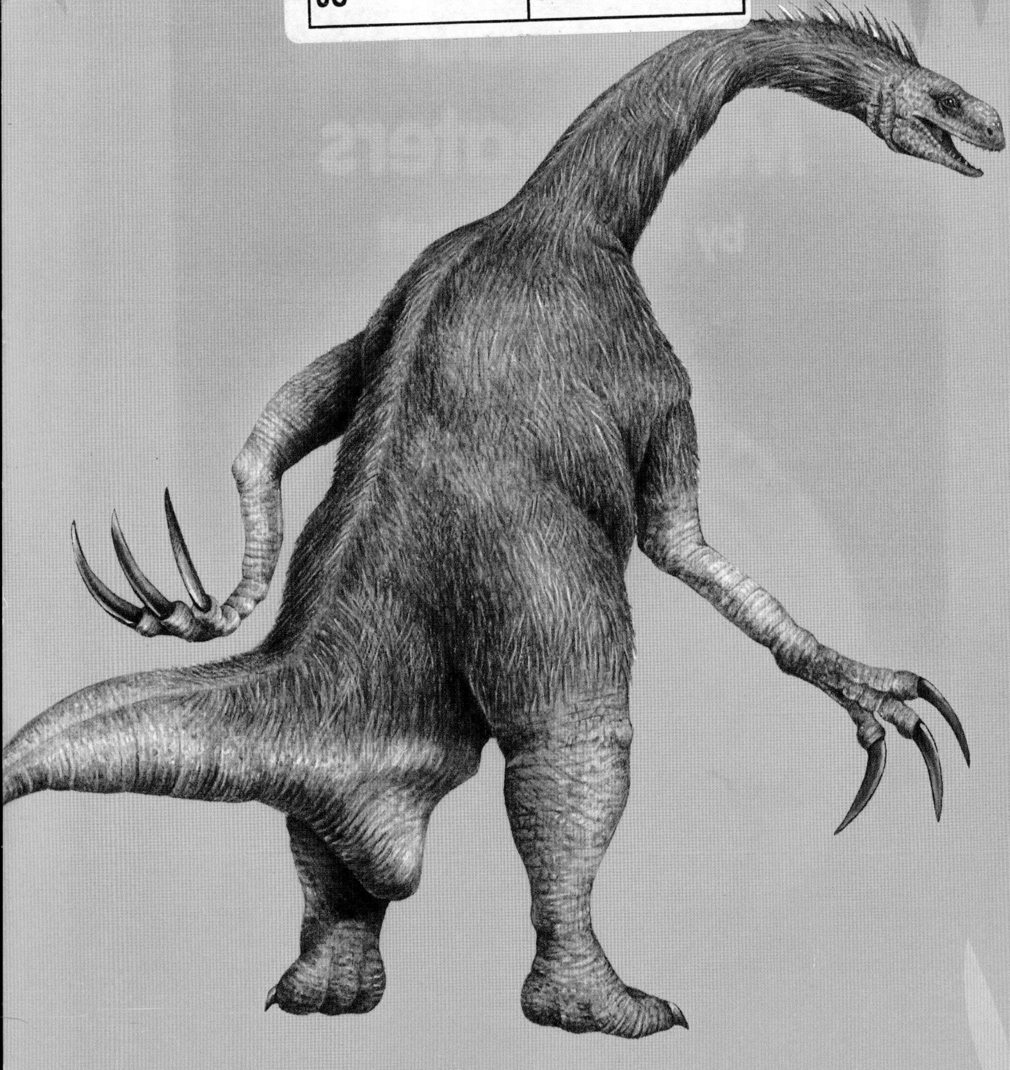

CONTENTS

Words in **bold** are explained in the glossary.

What did dinosaur hunters look like?

Dinosaur hunters had big heads.

They had sharp teeth.

They had little arms.

4

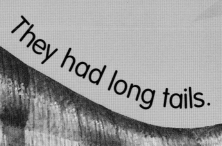

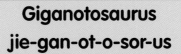

Giganotosaurus
jie-gan-ot-o-sor-us

They had long tails.

They had long legs.

How big were they?

Some dinosaur hunters were small.

Compsognathus
comp-sog-nay-thuss

Size

This dinosaur was
the size of a cat.

Some dinosaur hunters were big.

Allosaurus
all-o-saw-russ

Size

This dinosaur was
nine metres long.

Dinosaur food

Dinosaur hunters were meat-eaters.

Tyrannosaurus rex
(tie-ran-o-sor-us rex)

8 Some dinosaur hunters ate other dinosaurs.

Some dinosaur hunters
ate other animals.

Dragonflies

Fish

Lizards

Hunting

Some dinosaurs hunted alone.

Dilophosaurus
dill-o-fo-saw-rus

They would kill small plant-eaters.

Some dinosaurs hunted in a group.
Together they attacked **prey** much
bigger than themselves.

They used their
sharp teeth.

They used their
big **claws**.

Deinonychus
die-non-ie-cuss

Tyrannosaurus rex

Tyrannosaurus rex ate other dinosaurs.

It had big teeth.

Tyrannosaurus rex
tie-ran-o-sor-us rex

It was fierce!

This is a T. rex **fossil**.

Size

T. rex means 'cruel king lizard'.

Deinonychus

This dinosaur ran very fast.

It ran after its prey.

It had very big claws.

It was very fierce.

Size

Deinonychus
die-non-ee-cus

This dinosaur's name
means 'terrible claw'.

Velociraptor

This dinosaur had feathers like a bird.

Its name means 'speedy thief'.

Velociraptor
vel-oss-ee-rap-tor

Size

It had a long tail.

It had very
big claws on
its back feet.

Segnosaurus

This dinosaur's name means 'slow lizard'.

Segnosaurus
seg-no-sor-us

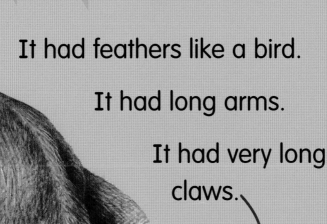

It had feathers like a bird.

It had long arms.

It had very long claws.

Coelophysis

These dinosaurs ate lizards and small dinosaurs.

They lived in big groups.

Coelophysis
see-lo-fie-sis

They had small arms and
long legs.

Size

Glossary

claws
Long, sharp
nails.

dinosaur
A lizard-like
animal that
lived millions
of years ago.

fossil
A very old skeleton
that has turned
into rock.

hunter

An animal that catches and kills other animals.

prey

Animals that are hunted and killed by others.

Index

Copyright © ticktock Entertainment Ltd 2008
First published in Great Britain in 2008 by ticktock Media Ltd.,
Unit 2, Orchard Business Centre, North Farm Road, Tunbridge Wells, Kent TN2 3XF
ISBN 978 1 84696 752 8 pbk
Printed in China

We would like to thank: Penny Worms, Shirley Bickler, Suzanne Baker and the National Literacy Trust.

Picture credits (t=top, b=bottom, c=centre, l-left, r=right, OFC= outside front cover)
Corbis: Page 13. Shutterstock: 22b. Dinosaur artwork: ticktock Media Ltd.